Evita: The Life of Eva Perón

By Charles River Editors

About Charles River Editors

Charles River Editors was founded by Harvard and MIT alumni to provide superior editing and original writing services, with the expertise to create digital content for publishers across a vast range of subject matter. In addition to providing original digital content for third party publishers, Charles River Editors republishes civilization's greatest literary works, bringing them to a new generation via ebooks.

Sign up here to receive updates about free books as we publish them, and visit Our Kindle Author Page to browse today's free promotions and our most recently published Kindle titles.

Introduction

Eva Perón (1919-1952)

María Eva Duarte de Perón, known to the world as Evita, stands with Jesus Christ as a highly influential historical figure who lived only 33 years. The similarities do not end there: as Argentine novelist Tomás Eloy Martínez has observed, Evita came to "symbolize certain naïve, but effective, beliefs: the hope for a better world; a life sacrificed on the altar of the disinherited, the humiliated, the poor of the earth . . . myths which somehow reproduce the image of Christ." During her life she was elevated to the status of "spiritual leader" of her country, Argentina, and after death she was regarded there as a martyr and a saint by her many followers. A visit to the museum dedicated to Evita's legacy in the Botánico neighborhood of Buenos Aires reveals the spirit of quasi-religious devotion that surrounds her: more than simply a collection of historical displays, the museum stands as a shrine to her legacy and intends to imbue its viewers with the spirit and beliefs of the deceased First Lady. In one of the rooms, the visitor stands in the presence of one of her most famous dresses in a centrally placed glass case, with the scent of roses artificially pumped into the air. Like many of the other objects, the dress is presented much as were the relics of medieval saint. Evita's tomb in the same city's Recoleta cemetery, constantly garlanded with fresh bouquets and notes of gratitude from pilgrims who have come to pay their respects, provides further evidence of her revered presence in Argentine culture.

At the same time, the presence of the major artifacts of Evita's person in these particular locations is also ironic and revealing of the great social divisions over which she presided.

Botánico is a prestigious and wealthy neighborhood, and the Recoleta is the burial place of Argentina's oligarchy; Eva Perón prided herself on having antagonized and earned the hatred of precisely these social classes. Over 50 years after her death, Perónism, the political philosophy devised by her and her husband Juan Domingo Perón, remains a potent force in Argentine politics (the current president identifies herself closely with the Peróns and their legacy), but it also continues to inspire deep enmity. While a large portion of the country sees Evita as a symbol of national pride, there is also a significant sector that sees her as an impostor and a demagogue whose brilliant but irresponsible manipulation of mass politics helped sink the country into chaos. Whereas some controversial political figures tend to become more broadly and neutrally admired as the distance from their lifespan grows, within her own country Evita remains as much a lightning rod as ever.

Since her death, the mythology and legend of Evita have grown monumentally. Though millions worshipped Eva, who nearly became the Vice-President of Argentina before her premature death, opinions of her still vary between two extremes. While some think of her as an angelic woman who sought to uplift women and the poor, others view her as a self-serving, egotistical, and embittered woman who used sex to rise up Argentina's social and political ladder and seek vengeance on the upper classes. *Evita: The Life of Eva Perón* humanizes the youngest of 5 siblings who once had more modest ambitions as Eva Duarte, and it explores the mythology and legacy that have grown around Evita, examining her representations in literature, film, and theatre to uncover the truth behind her enigmatic existence.

Chapter 1: Evita's Early Years

Eva at her First Communion in 1926

María Eva Duarte was born in Los Toldos, an agricultural town in the province of Buenos Aires, on May 7, 1919. She was the fifth child of Juana Ibaguren and Juan Duarte, a wealthy landowner, but Duarte and Ibaguren were not married; in fact, Duarte kept a legitimate wife and family in another nearby town, Chivilcoy. In her autobiography and elsewhere, Evita stated that her second-class status as an illegitimate child, including regular taunting with the epithet of "bastard", helped consolidate her sense of identification with the country's oppressed classes. Allegedly, when Duarte died, his wife and relatives attempted to exclude Juana and her children from the funeral, but the circumstances of the event are controversial. Either way, while he was alive, Duarte neglected his second family with Juana despite his economic capacity to keep them comfortable, so Eva grew up in poverty despite being the daughter of an oligarch. Things grew worse after Juan Duarte's death in a car accident in 1926, leaving the family with no support. They moved to the larger town of Junín in 1930, which gave them greater economic and educational opportunities.

While Eva's family experienced its own personal turmoil, the years during Eva's childhood were years of seismic political changes in Argentina. The traditional landed oligarchy, whose wealth was based on the exportation of grains and meat to Europe, was facing major political challenges from demographically emergent political classes, especially after the electoral reform of 1912 created universal male suffrage. Beginning in 1916, the Radical Party, representative of the urban middle class with some working class support, had been in control of the national government and had made inroads in the provinces, including the area of Buenos Aires Province where Eva grew up.

The population explosion of the urban working class presented a major challenge to the ruling parties, especially since Italian and Spanish immigrants had brought with them socialist, anarchist, and syndicalist ideals and set out organizing trade unions among the previously politically marginal immigrant laboring population. The year of Eva's birth also witnessed a major strike in Buenos Aires that led to violent government repression and many deaths, a series of events that became known as the *semana trágica*.

However, the Radical governments that ruled from 1916-1930, the period of Eva's childhood, proved themselves largely incapable of keeping their coalition together or of addressing the discontent of the urban poor. Their failure led to a return to power by conservatives, but that was an equally unsatisfying arrangement for much of the population. Together, these events created a power vacuum that would ultimately be filled by Perónism.

Initially, Eva's early ambitions were artistic, not political. As a schoolgirl, she loved singing and reciting poetry, and after the family moved to Junín she became involved in school plays and other amateur theatrics. Junín was a large enough town to have a cinema, and she fell in love with the glamour of the movies at a time when Argentina was mainly importing Hollywood productions for local screenings. Most of her sisters had settled to cook, keep house, and sew, and one was a teacher, one of the more honored professions available to women in that time and place, but Eva's ambitions were too great to be fulfilled by a conventional provincial life, and she announced as much to her family and the authorities at her school. Although she faced reluctance from her mother in particular, in 1934, the 15 year old teen made her way to Buenos Aires for an audition to appear on a radio station. The circumstances of her departure are unclear, with some accounts claiming that she ran away from home in the company of an older musician, and others asserting that her mother accompanied her on her initial move to the city. Whatever, the case, she never looked back, and she would remain based in the capital for the rest of her life.

One of Eva's biographers described Buenos Aires during this time: "Buenos Aires in the 1930s was the continent's most cosmopolitan and elegant metropolis, and soon became known as the 'Paris of South America.' As in any great European capital, the center of the city was filled with cafés, restaurants, theaters, movie houses, shops, and bustling crowds. In direct contrast to the glamour of the city, the 1930s were also years of great unemployment, poverty, and hunger in the capital, and many new arrivals from the interior were forced to live in tenements, squalid boardinghouses, and in outlying shantys that became known as villas miserias."

All in all, Eva's upbringing makes her a surprising figure to become the political champion of Argentina's urban working class. Provincial and descended from old Spanish stock, she had little exposure to the very different Argentina that had sprung up in the capital over the previous decades as the result of immigration, population growth, and industrialization. One can just as easily imagine her making good use of her descent from a wealthy landed family, as well as her pale complexion (Buenos Aires society was highly racist), to augment her reputation and social class.

Chapter 2: An Actress in Buenos Aires

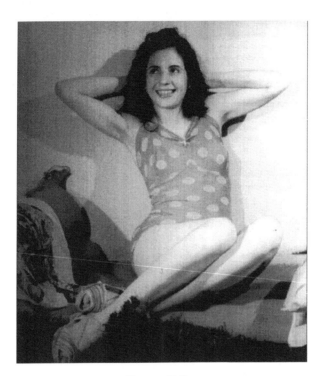

20 year old Eva

During Eva's early years, Argentina was changing culturally as well as politically, not least because of the rise of a mass culture of entertainment, a development that would define Eva's career as both an actress and political leader. There was a new, and growing, audience for entertainment of all kinds, as opposed to earlier eras when opera, theater, and classical music had been luxuries of the moneyed classes. When Eva went to Buenos Aires, she was only one of many young women and men who hoped to make their way within this economy. Despite a relative lack of connections or serious training, she would succeed in surprisingly short order.

Shortly after arriving in the capital, Eva obtained work with a touring theatrical troupe called the Compañía Argentina de Comedia, playing minor parts for a small salary. She received some positive reviews in the press and became something of a known entity on the theatrical circuit, which subsequently allowed her to obtain work for a more prestigious company. Eva appeared mainly in popular drama, a form of entertainment that was still competing for viewers with the cinema. Buenos Aires in this period remained the sophisticated, culturally vibrant place it had become in the high period of Argentina's wealth in the early 20th century, when architects and urban planners did their best to make the city look and feel like Paris. Thus, there were large markets for all forms of entertainment among the wide array of social classes that made up the population. On the other hand, the Great Depression in the U.S. and Europe had left the agriculture-oriented Argentine countryside devastated, and many poor rural residents had flocked to the city, adding to the poor masses and creating a mood of social tension between the wealthy and middle-class residents of older stock and the poor immigrants from the interior and abroad.

Attempting to make it in a crowded city where money and resources were scarce tested the resilience of the young aspiring actress, who was forced to live with meager resources in austere conditions. Years later, once she had become well-known enough to be interviewed by an entertainment magazine, Eva described her first years as an actress as "five years of troubles, of noble struggles when I've known the uncertainty of adversity as well as the gratification of success." This interview, which came prior to her self-refashioning as a political icon, indicates she was beginning to identify with her audience by comparing her own story to the "struggles" of the average Argentine.

By 1937, Eva was finding greater success, including her first appearances on the radio and on the cinema screen, both growing forms of entertainment that were coming into their own by the end of the decade. This also helped her expand her chances of getting new roles on the stage, in the movies, and on radio dramas. She appeared in four or five melodramatic movies from the later 1930s to the mid-1940s, which were comparable to B-list movies, but her greatest successes were with the radio station Radio Belgrano. Eva participated in and eventually spearheaded a number of highly popular programs, including radio soap operas and a series of historical dramas called "Biographies of Illustrious Women," in which Eva played a number of famous personages such as Queen Elizabeth I. It is tempting to conclude that she was already "trying out" for her own historic role.

Eva Duarte and Libertad Lamarque in the musical film *La cabalgata del circo*.

It was on these radio programs that Eva later felt she reached the "height of her career" in acting, and it was through the fame that she achieved as a radio actress that she ended up undergoing a major career change by way of the most fateful encounter of her life. In 1944, an earthquake devastated the Argentine city of San Juan, and the government's labor and social welfare minister, Colonel Juan Domingo Perón, had the idea of enlisting the country's best known entertainers in the relief effort. They used their fame to solicit donations from the public for the earthquake victims, holding a charity gala to raise funds at the city's largest venue, Luna Park.

Luna Park in Buenos Aires today

Juan Perón

It was at this event that Eva met Perón, 25 years her senior, who had been appointed labor minister by the military government that had ousted President Ramón Castillo in a coup in 1943. He was still not a widely known figure, but he had used his role to develop close relationships with trade union leaders and had developed social welfare programs that had won him the admiration and loyalty of many poor Argentines. In the aftermath of the earthquake and the charitable drives, Perón was elevated to the status of Vice President in the military government. His fame and popularity was on the rise.

According to most accounts, Eva left the Luna Park gala with Perón, and they were inseparable from then on. Meanwhile, Eva began to promote Perón's cause by using the resources available to her in her work. For one, she helped spearhead and became president of a union for radio employees. At the same time, she created a radio program dedicated to narrating the progress achieved by the current government, especially under Perón's direction.

President Farrell and Vice President Perón in 1945

The use of the media to solidify popular support for the government was probably a crucial element of Perón's political survival during this period. The older military officers involved in the government were becoming wary of the younger upstart, as well as the power base he was in the process of building through patronage relationships with trade unions. Perón's status was inferior in the military hierarchy, but he had won the fervent loyalty of many of the young officers, and he was now buffering his position with new bases of support. Among the members of this government, which had come into power by force, only Perón was perceived as having a certain legitimacy through popular support, and those who were uncomfortable with his meteoric ascent to power knew that they risked spurring a popular revolt if they attempted to depose him. Eva, now Perón's constant companion and public champion, would inevitably become a player in the turmoil surrounding him, and thus one of the most dramatic historical turns Argentina had ever witnessed.

Perón and Eva

Chapter 3: The Rise of Evita

After the tensions had mounted for over a year, matters played out precisely as Perón's opponents had feared. By the final months of 1945, his popularity had soared, and it seemed inevitable that he would seize control of the military government if permitted to remain in power. His enemies organized a coup against him, arresting him on October 9 and stripping him of his ministries and titles. He was taken away from Buenos Aires and imprisoned on a small island controlled by the military. When the news of these events spread, his tireless work with the trade unions paid off, as these and allied organizations organized a mass rally in front of the Presidential Palace to demand Perón's release. The rally attracted hundreds of thousands of supporters, making the military rulers realize that they were at risk of a full-scale revolution. The protestors refused to disband until Perón appeared free in front of them, and his captors finally relented, realizing how much more skillfully their nemesis had played his hand. Late on the night of October 17, Perón appeared on the balcony of the Casa Rosada, announcing to his cheering supporters that elections would soon be held.

Protesters calling for Perón's release on October 17, 1945.

The Casa Rosada (Pink House) today

While popular accounts have claimed that Eva played a role in organizing the protests that resulted in Perón's release, this is probably unlikely. However, her connection to Perón's political destiny was already sealed, and this would be made official just five days after the colonel's release from imprisonment, when the two married in a civil ceremony (followed up with a religious ceremony a few months later).

This was regarded even by Perón's supporters as a dubious move: Perón had been previously married, so he would now have the stigma of being a remarried divorcé in a conservative Catholic country. On top of that, his new wife was an illegitimate child from a poor background, and, worst of all, an actress, a profession associated with sexual promiscuity in the popular mind. Members of Perón's inner circle of military supporters viewed the marriage as a lapse of judgment and discipline that could bring about disastrous political consequences, but this would clearly prove a serious misdiagnosis. As it turned out, Eva's humble background and the scorn she attracted from conservative elites created sympathy for her among millions of Argentines, and her familiarity as a radio and film star strengthened the popular sympathy she was able to elicit. Even Perón himself could not have anticipated just how valuable a political ally he had enlisted.

Elections were scheduled for February 1946, and Perón campaigned tirelessly as the candidate of the Labor Party, whipping up the resentment of the poor working classes (the so-called *descamisados*) against the country's traditional governing class. But Perón also gained solid support among middle class Argentines who were tired of the chaos and incompetence of previous governments and inspired by Perón's nationalistic pride and fervor. He promised to make the country more economically independent, foment the growth of local industry, and strengthen social protections in health, education, and pensions. While he had visited and been inspired by Mussolini's corporatist state in Italy, Perón also made great efforts to appeal to the left wing of the working class, within which a strong Communist movement had failed to take hold.

Eva used her radio presence to trumpet her husband's achievements and promises to a country highly receptive to her dramatic style and frequent allusions to her own humble origins and struggles. She also accompanied Perón to campaign events and began to establish herself as a formidable political force on the podium as well. Ultimately, it was for her speeches rather than her radio transmissions that she was most remembered, and it was during the campaign that she began to be referred to (at her own encouragement) by the diminutive "Evita", a term of popular affection that would accompany her status as a public mother-protector figure.

Juan Perón won the February election with 56% of the vote, a commanding victory that gave him a free hand to pursue his policies, which sought a nationalistic drive for autonomy and economic power, as well as the creation of an expansive welfare state. Although she held no official position in his government, Evita played a major role in the latter effort in particular, acting as a liaison between the government and poor communities and a promoter of government policies. She also created the Fundación Eva Perón, a charitable entity supported by the government and private donations that offered a wide array of services, especially to women and children.

Evita meets with children while working in the Eva Perón Foundation.

As a result, Evita became the public face of the government's social and economic policy, overseeing improvements in health care services, education, child care, care for the elderly, and helping to negotiate improved wages and benefits for the country's major unions. She also made a major drive to expand suffrage to women, an effort that succeeded with the passage of a law extending the vote to adult women in 1947. Though outspoken in her devotion to the Catholic faith, Evita was held in suspicion and contempt by the Catholic hierarchy, which disliked the example she was setting for women and found her self-posturing as a saint to be inappropriate, especially given what they regarded as her impure background. But she had earned the devotion of much of the population, and as much as her detractors may have despised her, there was little they could do to stop her, just as they had been hard-pressed to curtail her husband's ambitions.

In June 1947, Eva set out on a tour of Europe, which was intended to gain allies for the new Argentine regime among the European countries and increase the international profile of the new leader through public appearances by his charismatic and photogenic wife. The trip reflected a number of political ironies surrounding the new regime. The first port of call was Madrid, where Evita was greeted warmly by General Francisco Franco, the country's right-wing dictator over the last 10 years. She visited the tombs of the "Catholic Monarchs", Ferdinand and Isabella, who had sponsored Christopher Columbus' historic voyage in 1492, and Evita received the Cross of

Queen Isabella from the government. There was a certain irony in Evita's warm welcome in fascist Spain, since Franco had come to power largely by crushing the country's powerful urban labor movements, the same kind of groups that formed Perón's strongest base of support in Argentina. The association of the Perón regime with fascism was highlighted again in Italy, where a gathering of Communists protested one of Evita's public appearances. She also made a visit to the Vatican, where the Pope presented her with a rosary. Finally, she visited France, a major buyer of Argentine grain, and met with Charles de Gaulle, another nationalist military officer who had reached the presidency. She was unable to meet with the British monarch as she wished, but nevertheless she became something of an international celebrity as major newspapers and magazines published pieces on her and increased her profile around Europe and in the U.S. Even a Time magazine profile of Evita appeared during her European tour.

Evita arriving in Madrid

Evita in Rome

Once back in Argentina, Evita set herself to organizing the women's movement within Perónism by founding a Partido Perónista Feminista (Perónist-Feminist Party) to organize women supporters into political and social action. Interestingly, the Perónist push for women's voting rights had not gained the support of the pre-existing feminist movement in Argentina, which was mainly composed of educated women of the upper and middle classes. In general, the educated classes of Argentina belonged to the starkly anti-Perón minority of the country's population, and they regarded the leader's every move with suspicion. In this case, they viewed the extension of suffrage to women as an attempt to lock in a new voting bloc in support of Perón, rather than to genuinely better the condition of women. Ironically, some of the outspoken women's rights advocates opposed the women's suffrage bill out of general opposition to Perón and Evita.

Evita speaking to women

The failure to develop an effective women's movement in Argentina in previous decades, when many other countries already achieved women's suffrage, had been partly the result of class divisions. Educated feminists had been unable to galvanize political involvement among the vast population of poor working women. Evita made for an unusual feminist because she still held traditional views about a woman's role in the household, and she was a model of subordinate devotion in her marriage to Perón, but she was far more successful in influencing the lower classes. Her organizing abilities created a powerful women's movement subordinate to Perónism but capable of achieving political ends to the benefit of women in general. The women's faction of Perónism also played a major role in creating a new social welfare network over the first few years of Perón's presidency.

The early years of Perón's presidency were highly successful, and they made him and Evita even more popular. With the economy buoyed by growing exports to Europe, where agricultural production had been devastated by World War II, wages grew for most workers and the government was able to follow up on its promises of a better life for the working class, a growth of local industry, and a nationalization of a number of previously private industries to increase state revenues and fund public works and welfare. In this period of prosperity, Perón's nearly godlike status in the national consciousness became deeply engrained, and his opponents despaired of ever being able to mount a successful campaign against him.

Meanwhile, Evita became more ferocious in her denunciations of the rich and powerful, and she increasingly self-identified with the *descamisados*. Evita consolidated her public status by traveling the country, overseeing charitable projects, and tending personally to the poor all the while. Her much-publicized visits with orphans, the sick, the destitute, and the elderly lent her the aura of a saint, tapping into Argentina's deeply Catholic sensibilities, even as her detractors attempted to draw attention to her previous career and viewed her current foray into political theater as simply a new and exciting way for her to continue her acting career.

Chapter 4: Perónism's First Challenges

Eva's official portrait in 1947

By 1949, what many had hoped was the Perónist economic miracle was beginning to look more like a bubble. Grain exports dropped due to more competition from the U.S. under the Marshall Plan, which essentially incentivized European purchases of American products.

Furthermore, a spike in grain and beef consumption within Argentina reduced the amount of agricultural products channeled into exports. As a consequence of these developments, the country entered a balance of payments crisis, particularly since the industrialization program spearheaded by Perón's government required the purchase of heavy machinery from the U.S., which in turn required dollars that the country was no longer able to obtain. The U.S. was happy to lend the country money to purchase its products, but this went against Perón's nationalist ideals, and it was something of an embarrassment given that he had just recently taken great pride in paying off Argentina's foreign debts. In the end, his government relented and took out a credit of $125 million to purchase materials needed for industrial growth, but these developments revealed that Argentina was still highly dependent on exports and highly vulnerable to small economic shifts around the globe. The ideal of national autonomy preached by the government was going to take much longer to achieve than had been imagined, and in the meantime the government was obliged to permit foreign investment and impose austerity measures in order to avoid economic crisis, moves which threatened to alienate key constituencies.

Over the next few years, Perón had to be more flexible in his economic policies than he might have liked, cutting deals with Standard Oil and other major corporations that seemed to violate the spirit of economic nationalism. On the other hand, he and Evita solidified what they presented as the regime's governing ideology, under the name of *Justicialismo*. The Labor Party, for which Perón was the candidate in 1945, was transformed into the Justicialist Party the following year. The Justicialist movement's central document was a manifesto containing "20 Truths" that guided the Party's political action, stating that "a government without a doctrine is a body without a soul. That is why Perónism has a political, economic, and social doctrine: Justicialism."

In reality, the manifesto seems to use the terms "Justicialism" and "Perónism" interchangeably. Essentially, the 20 Truths emphasize popular collective political action, nationalism, work, and social justice. Alluding to Evita's extra-governmental work in her Foundation, the document states that "the two arms of Perónism are Social Justice and Social Welfare. With them we give the People our embrace of justice and love." It also echoes Evita's frequent sanctification of children in her social work: "In the New Argentina the only privileged ones are the children." Articulating Perón's economic doctrines, it states that capital should be placed at the service of general social welfare. Justicialism, the document also claims, is not just a political doctrine but "a new philosophy of life, simple, practical, popular, profoundly Christian and profoundly humanist."

Justicialism was an eclectic political philosophy that amalgamated a variety of different political creeds, including nationalism, socialism, fascism, and Catholic social teaching. It was clearly intended to include as wide an array of the ideological spectrum as possible, while maintaining a few basic, uniting doctrines. But as the term "Perónism" itself implies, it was difficult to separate the doctrine from the two charismatic leaders who promulgated it. On one hand, this meant that a fervent personal loyalty was tantamount to a fervent political loyalty from a large sector of the population, meaning that people still supported Perón even when things were not going well. But on the other hand, Perónism meant the suspicion and hatred directed at both Juan and Evita Perón by opponents did not diminish as they became more familiar either.

After the discouraging economic developments of 1949-1950, the government began to respond to the fierce criticisms of the opposition by imposing stricter controls on free speech and by limiting the independence of sources of opposition, including among the press and the universities. A new law of *desacato* (disrespect) allowed critics of the government to be prosecuted and imprisoned, while opposition publications had limits placed on their expression and production. In some cases, opposition papers were even taken over by the government. There was an attempt to "Perónize" all of society, placing a wider range of institutions in direct subservience to the Justicialist Party and the state organisms it controlled. Perón's continued sway over much of the army provided a further way to keep the country firmly in his grasp.

Not surprisingly, Perón's overreach galvanized opposition to his rule in new sectors, including the Church and parts of the military, not the kinds of enemies he wanted to contend with when elections were coming up in 1951. And certain limits on his power were evident in the problematic attempt of Evita herself to stand as Vice President with him in those elections. While her fervent supporters among the general populace were encouraging her strongly in this direction, Juan's military allies were by and large hostile to this idea, and he knew that he needed to maintain their loyalty.

In the run-up to the 1951 election, there was a massive rally of two million supporters in downtown Buenos Aires, at which both Peróns gave speeches. When Evita spoke, the crowd chanted its demand that she announce her vice presidential candidacy, but she held off from doing so, promising them she would come to a decision within days. A few days later, she turned to her favored medium of old, the radio, to issue the announcement that she would not join her husband's political ticket. Her eloquent renunciation only further strengthened her reputation as a woman of honor and integrity, and it has gone down in history as one of her most famous orations. In reality, though, she may have been prevented from running by expedient considerations on the part of her husband and his campaign. In the end, Perón easily trounced his opponent in the 1951 campaign with a commanding 63% of the vote, thanks in part to a strong level of support from the recently enfranchised women organized by Evita into the Partido Perónista Feminista.

The rally with an estimated 2 million supporters.

Evita hugging Juan after speaking at the rally.

Official portrait of the Peróns, 1948. Perón was the first president to appear in an official portrait with his wife.

There was a further dimension to the controversy surrounding Evita's candidacy for the vice presidency, but it was one that hardly anyone, including her, understood at the time. Evita had been experiencing fainting spells, fatigue and other unsettling symptoms since 1950, and it finally led her to seek medical advice. After that, she was diagnosed with cervical cancer, a diagnosis that was withheld from her by her own husband and doctors for a time. This was a common practice when a patient received a possibly terminal diagnosis. The public was unable to obtain much information on her health and was regularly informed that there was nothing seriously wrong with their "spiritual leader."

Great efforts were made to keep up public appearances, but Evita began to find herself unable to maintain the demanding regime of travel, charity work, and political campaigning that had become central to her life in the past few years. In late 1951, she underwent a hysterectomy in order to prevent the spread of the cancer, but it put her body under enormous stress without achieving that desired end. She also received a course of chemotherapy, which at the time was a form of treatment never used previously in Argentina, but all of the resources Evita's powerful husband brought to bear on her illness were to no avail. By the time he was about to assume his second term in office in the middle of 1952, she was on the brink of death.

In this October 1951 picture, Juan had to hold Evita up because she was too weak to stand on her own.

Evita's final speech to the public occurred on May Day of 1952, the key holiday of the Argentine labor movement for which she had become the lodestar and mother figure. It was her first speech in some time, as her severe health problems and the disappointment surrounding her failed bid for candidacy had combined to remove her somewhat from the limelight. Her May Day speech was one of the fiercest and most combative of her entire career. She denounced Perón's political enemies as "vipers" and "sellers of the fatherland" who "serve their masters of the foreign metropoli and handover the people of their own country to these masters with the same heartlessness with which they have sold out their country and their consciences." She made a plea to God that "He not permit these fools to lift their hands against Perón because –

¡woe to that day! – I will set out with the working people, I will set out with the women of the people, I will set out with the *descamisados* of the fatherland, and we will leave no brick unturned that is not *Perónista*." "I want the traitors out there to know," she added, "that we will take justice into our own hands if necessary." It is unclear whether she knew that her final day was approaching, but these ferocious final promises, pleas, and threats were delivered as if she knew her followers would have to act without her direction in the future. The speech consolidated the fanatical devotion of her followers, which would last well beyond her death. In equal measure, its threats of mob violence stoked the fears of her enemies, who would come to despise her as much in death as in life.

Just over a month later, on June 4, there was a public parade in celebration of the inauguration of Perón's second term in office. Evita accompanied him, but according to reports she was so weak that she had to be held up by a hidden frame and heavily dosed with painkillers during the prolonged public appearance. She gave no speech, and it turned out to be her last public appearance. Less than two months after the inaugural parade, on the night of July 26, she died. One doctor noted near the end, "If her spirit seemed to pass as lucid and vibrant to the end, her body had reduced itself to just the linings of her lacerated viscera and bones. It seems that all is left are 33 kilos of a lady who had once been so strong and rooted in this life..."

The news of Evita's death was immediately transmitted on the radio, the medium she had made such effective use of, and the entire country knew within a short time. The broadcast announced, "The Secretary of Information of the Presidency of the Nation carries out the excruciating duty of informing the people of the Republic that at 8:25 pm, Lady Eva Perón, Spiritual Leader of the Nation, has passed away."

The outpouring of grief was overwhelming, with flowers decking the area around the presidential palace and the surrounding streets within a short time. The body was made available for public viewing at the congressional building a few blocks away, and there were near riots as it was moved between the two buildings, with hundreds of thousands of devotees clamoring to be near what had taken on the status of a sacred relic. She was given a state funeral and a religious funeral, and Perón's government made plans to embalm the body and display it publicly in perpetuity, as had been done with that of the Soviet premier Vladimir Lenin, within a public monument dedicated to her.

Evita's funeral attracted an estimated 3 million people.

Evita's active and remarkable life as an entertainer-turned-political organizer and leader was like few the world had ever known, but she has had an equally dramatic second life. Her legacy has served as a constant presence in Argentine politics, and even her body has experienced a strange and mysterious course. The twists and turns of her political afterlife would reflect the vicissitudes of the ideology and movement she helped create.

Given the fate Perón's government suffered in the wake of his wife's death, it was not at all clear that the Perónist ideology would continue to thrive as it has. In his second term, without Evita by his side, the combative leader gained more enemies than he could handle, with particular opposition growing among the military and the Catholic Church, which had always been suspicious of him but with which he now openly clashed over secularization of schools, the legalization of divorce, and other matters. Ultimately, he was excommunicated as a result of these conflicts, as well as rumors surrounding his womanizing. In June 1955, in a spectacular coup attempt, military aircraft directed by officers in revolt bombarded a Perónist rally on the Plaza de Mayo outside the presidential palace, killing hundreds. The coup failed, but it was followed shortly after by another attempt, now led by a powerful coalition of conservative military officers who drove Perón out of the country. Perón fled to neighboring Paraguay under the protection of that country's dictator, Alfredo Stroessner.

The military junta that ruled the country for the following three years banned the Perónist ideology and organizations, forcing many supporters underground, and even the very mention of the names of Juan and Evita was illegal for a time. When elections were finally held in 1958, Perón was in exile in Madrid, and his followers were forbidden to vote for him or other Perónists. Nevertheless, he managed to exert influence from afar by instructing his followers to support the Radical Party candidate, Arturo Frondizi. The results demonstrated his continued clout: Frondizi won.

The story of the 1960s and 1970s in Argentina was in large measure the story of the conservative Argentine military's various attempts to control the polarizing political forces its wayward son, Juan Perón, had unleashed. After Frondizi served his term, the next elections elevated Arturo Illia to the presidency. In this election too, Perón and his followers played a significant role despite their official exclusion from participation. But after two years into Illia's term, he was deposed in another coup. Power was handed back and forth between the military and elected governments in a chaotic period that followed over the next decade. In 1973, the Perónist parties were finally permitted to run candidates in an election, and Perón's follower Héctor Cámpora won the presidency, with Perón's support from a distance. Finally, Perón himself was permitted by Cámpora's own decree to return to the country. New elections were declared, which he won with 63% of the vote.

Perón began his third term in office in October 1973, but his health was frail, and his own movement, despite its apparent success, was in serious disarray. This was partly a consequence of the internal ideological divisions that had marked it from the beginning. As he plotted his return to Argentina in the late 1960s and early 1970s, Perón inadvertently exacerbated these tensions by encouraging the growth of extreme left-wing and extreme right-wing factions of Perónism, under the assumption that widening his base of support would assure him a third victory. However, the internal conflicts of Perónism turned violent, with the left-wing *Montonero* faction of young radicals and the right-wing faction of conservative and nationalist military officers facing off in street fights and riots, each claiming the true mantle of Perónism.

Perón died less than a year after the beginning of his third term and never lived to see the final collapse of his dreams in the disastrous government of his third wife, Isabel Perón, who sided with the rightist faction of Perónism and spearheaded the campaign of extrajudicial killings against leftist opponents. Her policies would continue under the military junta that overthrew her in 1976.

Evita has persisted as a crucial presence in Perónist politics in Argentina, which remains a potent political force to this day. All of the long-serving presidents of Argentina in the past two decades have been Perónists, and the two most recent presidents, Néstor Kirchner and Cristina Fernández de Kirchner, have invited comparisons with the Peróns themselves on several grounds. They are a couple who have effectively ruled together, they have generally maintained a strong level of support from the country's working class, and after Argentina's 2001 financial crisis, they successfully resuscitated the original Perónist rhetoric of economic nationalism by denouncing foreign capital and nationalizing large sectors of the economy. Cristina Fernández has been called by some a "second Evita," a comparison she has generally denied, even while making effective political use of Evita's image.

Néstor and Cristina Kirchner

If anything, the financial woes of Argentina around the turn of the millennium, widely blamed on exploitative and reckless foreign banking and investment, have made Evita's nationalist appeals even more potent than they might have been in previous decades. Whatever the case, a visit to contemporary Argentina reveals the omnipresence of images of Evita as a national icon and quasi-saintly figure; there have even been efforts to persuade the Vatican to canonize her, but so far they have been unsuccessful.

Alongside the strange history of post-Evita Perónism, a second and even stranger drama unfolded surrounding her body. For some time after the coup of 1955, it was unclear what had happened to her body, which after her funeral had been embalmed and placed on display in the headquarters of the major union organization. After the coup, her body vanished. It was later revealed that the military leaders, wishing to deprive Perónism of its most potent symbol, had stolen the body and had it shipped to Italy, where it was left buried in an unmarked grave for nearly 20 years. One of the more bizarre incidents of terrorism carried out in the rising chaos of the early 1970s was the kidnapping of General Pedro Aramburu by the Montoneros, who revered Evita. They chose Aramburu in part because he had helped oversee the removal of her body away from Argentina, and they hoped to force the information of her resting place out of him. The attempt failed, and Aramburu was killed.

After the re-legalization of Perónism in 1971, the military revealed Eva's location to Perón, still in Spain, and he had her body brought to him at his residence in Madrid, where it remained until after his death. When he died, his wife and successor Isabel placed his body on display, and Isabel arranged for the transportation of Evita's body from Spain to Argentina. It was placed on display along with Perón's coffin in his residence on the outskirts of Buenos Aires. One may speculate that Isabel, a little-known figure attempting to lead a violently divided country, was hoping some of the symbolic potency of her late husband and her predecessor would be transmitted to her by way of this shrine. But in the long run, the effort did not pay off politically. She, like her husband before her, was deposed in a military coup in 1976, and the junta that would rule Argentina for nearly a decade afterwards once again banned and repressed Perónism.

As for Eva Perón's well-traveled body, the new military leaders ended its wanderings (presumably) forever. They arranged for her burial in the Duarte family tomb in the prestigious Recoleta cemetery. Even this act was not without controversy, since the Recoleta is traditionally the resting place of Argentina's oligarchs, the very class Eva spent her career antagonizing.

Evita's grave

Chapter 6: Eva Perón in Film

"I will return and be millions." – Evita, 1952

Even after the return of her body to Buenos Aires in 1976, another mystery arose: the discovery of the real Eva Perón. Her posthumous representations are numerous, and any artist, author or filmmaker who has tried to capture Evita Perón has shown a different aspect of what people assume to be her personality.

Instead of shedding light on who exactly this enigmatic person was, many of the representations only enforce a myth that they attempt to elucidate. In many artists' efforts to explain who she was, they have further expanded the mythology that continues to distance the world from the real Eva. This is the phenomenon of Eva Perón, the woman whose memory carries on as strong as ever in the collective consciousness of Argentina.

The most notable representations of Eva Perón, the woman who wanted to be a stage actress, have taken place on the silver screen. Two of the most important films that tackle the myth of Eva Perón, albeit in very different ways, are Allan Parker's musical *Evita* (1996), with music by

Andrew Lloyd Webber, and Juan Carlos Desanzo's film *Eva Perón* (1996). The first is the portrayal of a vindictive woman seeking fame, admiration and recognition, while the second focuses on her political life. Both develop the features that were key images to Eva's life, including her poor background, her early career as an actress, her desire to be famous, her relationship with her husband, her effusive speeches before thousands of people, her resentment against the aristocracy of Argentina, and her tragic death. In many ways, the Argentine film is a response to the American effort to dismantle her myth. But like the American film, *Eva Perón* captures only a narrow aspect of Eva's supposed personality.

The musical *Evita* shows a darker side of Eva Perón's personality. The film opens with a scene from her childhood where Eva waits with her mother and siblings outside of her father's funeral. There, the middle-class side of her father's family refuses to allow the lower class Eva and her siblings, who they consider as "illegitimate" offspring of the father, to enter. However, Eva pushes forward and runs to her father's casket. It is not long before strangers carry the crying Eva away from her father's corpse.

This event has an important impact on the anti-elitist Eva that the musical portrays. It also explains many of the choices that she makes later in the film, including her desire to move from the countryside to Buenos Aires, her willingness to take advantage of men to rise up the social ladder of Argentine society and, finally, her intention to displace the elites with the foundation she eventually establishes.

While *Evita* is not necessarily a legitimate representation of the true Eva Perón, it is a legitimate representation of her myth. Parker seeks to humanize Eva, showing her humble origins, the source of her vengeance, and her nature, which is vindictive, egocentric, and vain. It is a depoliticized representation of Eva that focuses on her personal qualities and the struggles she has with the nature of a class-based society. It is not a representation that portrays Eva as someone who genuinely wants to generate political change in order to help the "shirtless" or poor. Instead, it is a simplified representation that focuses on her superficial and sexual side. While many criticize its value, *Evita* still has worth as a lens for learning about the possible reasons behinds Eva's actions and why she chose the life she led.

Casting the role of Eva sparked considerable controversy, particularly when Allan Parker decided to make Madonna his leading woman. Many of the musical's critics felt that Madonna only added to the disengagement with politics and Argentine culture, reaffirming Eva as nothing but a superficial, visual object. One critic, Nina Gerassi-Navarro, specifically stated that "the choice of Madonna as lead actress brings her sexuality to the fore. Madonna trivializes the national and historical specificity of Evita, because she is a pop cultural icon characterized by superficiality. It is this shallowness that is the source of Eva's extraordinary visibility and plasticity."

However, this opinion only represents one side about the choice of Madonna to play Eva.

Madonna, while an actress and a pop cultural icon, was and still is one of the most powerful women in the entertainment industry, not to mention one of the most economically successful women in the world. In many ways, Madonna held and continues to hold the same kind of fame that Eva Perón did during her time. Also, a number of parallels justified the choice of Madonna, including Madonna's economic struggles when she was younger, the early death of a parent, a meteoric economic ascent, being thrust into the public eye, combined public resentment and admiration that contributed to her fame, and a general misunderstanding of who she is.

These commonalities help explain why Parker decided to cast Madonna in the role, as he wanted to use the star to capture the kind of spectacle that existed during the Perónist political movement. As is known, Eva was an integral part of the populist Perónist campaign, and she became famous for her material interests, sensational speeches in the main plaza of Buenos Aires (Plaza de Mayo) and on the radio, and her cult-like propaganda images in advertisements and textbooks.

In *Evita*, Parker takes advantage of another star, Antonio Banderas, who plays the role of Che Guevara. Banderas develops the myth of Eva when he sings, "Oh what a circus, oh what a show. Argentina has gone to town over the death of an actress called Eva Perón." In many ways, Perónism was a show and, no doubt, Eva was a central to its persistence.

As a response to Allan Parker's representation, Juan Carlos Desanzo captures another side of the myth with his film *Evita Perón*. The film addresses the political side of Evita, examining her desire to be the vice president of the nation, her negotiations with Argentina's workers' unions, and her powerful speeches in front of thousands of people in the Plaza de Mayo. Desanzo also highlights the important role that Eva played in constructing her foundation for the poor. The film captures Eva working at the Foundation every day in order to serve the poor, a critical aspect of her life that is absent from Parker's musical.

Additionally, Desanzo chose a main actress who did not have the same connotations as Madonna. With the choice of Esther Goris to play Eva, Desanzo opted for a more credible physical representation of Eva Perón. Goris has a strong voice and talks with a Buenos Aires accent, emphasizing the regional "che," especially when talking to her husband. In discussions between Eva and Juan Perón, the viewer not only sees the physical parallels between Eva Perón and Goris, but also more of the historical context that influenced her political thought. For example, when Eva Perón explains the reasons why she wants to be vice president, she tells her husband: "I was always an illegitimate, Juan, a bastard, I never had a right to anything. Well, that's it! Now, I want to be part of the state, I have the right, Juan...I want the vice presidency...I want that right." The film delves into similar themes as the musical, such as the funeral scene and Eva's "illegitimacy," but it also explores the more profound reasons for Eva's actions and decisions. The film does not portray her as a purely vindictive woman who uses other people to social climb within Argentine society, but rather as a passionate and dynamic woman who understands the significance of her role in changing the lives of Argentines and impacting the life of her husband.

Another aspect that adds to the film's professional and political representation is the title itself. The decision to call the film *Eva Perón* was made to link the film immediately with a sense of neutrality and seriousness. On the other hand, the title for the musical *Evita* is the diminutive name that the poor of Argentina gave to Eva. Although Parker does not portray an Eva who necessarily deserved to be called by that term of endearment, the name lends her representation a sense of superficiality and deceit. Desanzo takes advantage of Eva's full name to avoid linking her with falsity or superficiality.

Chapter 7: Eva Perón in Literature

One aspect of the myth of Eva Perón that has been a source of theories and artistic inspiration does not necessarily have to do with Eva while she was alive, but rather her death. The circumstances of her death and what happened to her body after the political downfall of Perón were important issues that influenced a new wave of literature that explored Eva's myth.

Of all the authors who were obsessed with the death of Eva Perón, those who wrote the best-known stories were Jorge Luis Borges, author of "El simulacro" (*The Sham,* 1960), and Rodolfo Walsh, who wrote "Esa mujer" (*That Woman,* 1965) In the first, Borges highlights the reaction to Eva's death in Chaco, a small town in the interior of Argentina. In his story, a mourner (which supposedly was Perón) comes to Chaco one day in July 1952 with a cardboard box. Inside the box is a blond-haired doll of Eva Perón. The doll served as symbol of Eva for the people of Chaco who could not afford to go to the funeral in Buenos Aires. Borges uses this mock funeral of a doll to play with the theme of falsity. He refers to the ceremony as "a funereal farce" and finally says, "The carrier was not Perón and the doll was not the woman Eva Duarte Perón, but neither was Perón Perón nor Eva Eva."

In just three paragraphs, Borges shares his interpretation of Perónism and the leading personalities of the movement. He establishes a relationship between Perónist politics and falsehood, a relationship that one can immediately see in the story's title. The doll is a false representation of Eva used to trick the people of Chaco into continuing their admiration for her and the Perónist party. The story's narrator states that there exists no real difference between the doll and the person, describing Eva's political life as nothing more than a trick to fool the masses. Apparently, this was the opinion of Borges, who thought that there was nothing of truth in the illusory life of Eva Perón.

In the story "That Woman," Rodolfo Walsh also looks at the subject of Evita's corpse. Walsh writes of an interview that allegedly happened between him and a Colonel "with a German surname." This refers to Moori Koenig, one of the military officials in charge of guarding Eva Perón's corpse after its disappearance. In actuality, Koenig was a necrophiliac who engaged in sexual acts with the corpse. When the government discovered what Koenig was doing with the body, officials relieved Colonel Koenig of his duties and replaced him with someone named

Hector Caballitas. In the story, a journalist looking for the body meets with Koenig, though he clarifies that Eva Perón means nothing to him. The truth is that the journalist is just as obsessed with the body as the Colonel. The journalist hates the Colonel and an underlying thought that runs through his mind is that the Colonel is deliberately keeping the body's location secret. While the journalist probes the Colonel for information, it is apparent that the Colonel has gone mad. Indications of the coronel's necrophiliac tendencies present themselves when he talks constantly about the nakedness of the body and refers to Eva as a goddess, demonstrating its morbid fascination with the body.

During the interview, the journalist becomes all the more certain that the Colonel knows where the body must be. But the Colonel does not really know why the government has taken the corpse away. By then, it is clear that the journalist is also going mad as a result of his obsession with resolving the mystery of the corpse. When the Colonel does not share the location of the corpse, the journalist says, "Are not you concerned with history? I write the story, and you'll look good…forever, Colonel!" The story ends with the Colonel saying: "It is mine. That woman is mine." The use of "that woman" in this sense refers to the body not only as an object or piece of property, but also in the sense of a wife belong to the husband as a piece of property.

An interesting theme that arises in "That Woman" is one of illness affecting those who are obsessed with Eva's corpse. Interestingly, the Colonel refers to the tomb of Tutankhamen during his conversation with the journalist. Many believe that Tutankhamen's tomb was curses, since its discovery led to unexplained illnesses and deaths of those who found it. The story plays with the idea that Eva's body can and never will be the property of anyone, and those who think otherwise will only find themselves experiencing grave consequences.

An author who portrays a very creative representation of Eva is Nestor Perlongher. In his work, *Evita Vive* (*"Evita Lives,"* 1989), he touches on several different topics: the fame, parties, the excess, drugs, homosexuality, and so on. Perlongher, who was an open homosexual, uses these aspects of life to show Eva as a confident and daring person with the qualities necessary for relating to the poor. While many literary works represent Eva as if she were an object of desire, Perlongher turns to the story around to focus on what she desires. Although this Eva want things like marijuana, drugs, intimate relationships with other women, etc., Perlongher writes not to propose a demeaning representation, but one that shows a more real and rooted quality in comparison to other inflated, mythological, or sanctified representations of Eva.

Chapter 8: Eva Perón in Theater

The fascination with Eva Perón that existed in literature eventually evolved, taking form on the stage in plays that also sought to dismantle her myth. The active dialogue of the character of Eva Perón has made it possible for the creation of more intimate representations of her that are not as easily accessible in literature.

Plays about Eva have focused more on the events of her life prior to her death rather than her death itself or the disappearance of her body. Two plays dealing with the period immediately before Eva's death are *Eva Perón* (1970) by COPI and *Evita y Victoria: Comedia patriótica en tres actos* (*Evita y Victoria Patriotic Comedy in Three Acts*, 1992) by Monica Ottino. These representations portray two opposing personalities that characterize Eva during her sickness and capture her political adeptness, her intellect, and her relations with others during this troubling time of her life.

In the play *Eva Perón*, COPI shows Eva in her last moments as a woman who has clearly gone mad. Eva bosses around her mother, her maid Ibiza, her nurse and even her husband, forcing them to stay at home with her until the time of her death. To all of the other characters in the play, this ridiculous situation is the equivalent of hell because it is so difficult to deal with this Eva. She is constantly yelling at her mother, a dramatic woman who just wants to know the code to the safe where Eva stores all of her money. The crazy Eva realizes this and yells at her mother to go to her room, much like an irate parent would do to a misbehaving child. Through this entertaining relationship and her interactions with other people in the house, Eva comes off as bossy and spoiled. Some of her demands, such as "Nurse! Come paint my nails!" or "Mom! Come keep me company!" reveal a difficult type of personality that has not existed in earlier representations. This is also an Eva without reason who remains obsessed with extravagance and wealth.

In this representation, COPI plays with the idea of a living corpse that screams at and insults the most intimate people in Eva's life. It is obvious that COPI is not trying to show Eva as she always was, but he wants to exploit the idea of a living body to reveal some aspects of her personality and myth. For example, even on the cusp of death, Eva remains concerned with her image, especially her nails. This connects to reality in the sense that Eva had actually requested for her nails to be painted red upon her death.

Another interesting aspect is the gender dynamic between this Eva and Perón. Eva calls her husband a coward, laughs at the migraine he suffers from, and accuses him of trying to poison her. COPI contrasts Eva – the living body with cancer who is full of a rare type of domineering and masculine energy – with an inferior-seeming and feminized representation of Perón, who cannot manage to get out of bed due to the headaches he suffers. It is possible that COPI is trying to show the fragile state of Perón's power before Eva's death – a power that he could not sustain by himself.

In his exploration of Eva and Perón's relationship with their exchanged gender roles, COPI also addressed the whoring aspect of Eva's myth. When the nurse answers "no" to a question that Eva asks about her virginity, Eva says, "That's much better. Life is very exciting you know?" She makes the comment as if to suggest that she was a promiscuous woman in the past, alluding to the deliberate use of her sexuality to rise in the ranks of Argentine society and politics.

At the end of the play, Eva's personality changes considerably. When she talks with her nurse and hands over her favorite dress and jewelry, it is as though Eva is trying to relive her role as mother of the *descamisados*, or poor citizens of Argentina. But then it becomes apparent that Eva only gives these things to the nurse so that she may be a young, cute, and living corpse to be used in place of the withered Eva. Together, Eva and her maid skill the nurse. The play ends with a formal speech by Perón to the public, in which he declares the death of Eva. Interestingly, COPI binds the death of Eva with a lie, which supports a metaphor that COPI establishes between Eva and her real relationship with the poor. That is, COPI uses the generosity that Eva displayed with the nurse to represent what Eva did with her foundation to help the poor – superficial hand-outs that only served to promote Eva's interests. In addition, COPI uses the murder of the nurse to symbolize the anti-Perónist sentiment that the Perón regime and Eva were a hypocrisy that really did nothing to give more political representation for the poor.

Like COPI's play, *Evita and Victoria* (1990) by Monica Ottino is based on Eva's last days when she was very sick and dying. The playwright presents an intelligent, articulate, and clever Eva with a political agenda, similar to the politicized image in Desanzo's film *Eva Perón*. On the other hand, Ottino makes use of the character Victoria Ocampo, an author of Argentina's high society, to question Eva's political ideology and to develop a thorough debate between the two. Through their conversations, Ottino reveals aspects that Parker presented in *Evita* – a woman inspired by vengeance and a desire to obtain more power as she manipulated the people of the middle and upper classes. Because Ottino did not focus on just one aspect of the myth of Eva Perón, she does not create a being that is surreal or unbelievable, but rather a human being with whom the viewer can relate.

During the first act, the conversation between Eva and Victoria contains several comments that reveal the characteristics of her personality that have been seen in previous representations. For example, Ottino takes advantage of the debate on women's suffrage to draw comments from Eva about the upper class.

> Eva: We have a common concern.
> Victoria: Really?
> Eva: Yes, the cause of women, women's suffrage, our lack of rights.
> Victoria: I'm an old fighter. But I think you've knocked on the wrong door. I'm not the only feminist of my generation, or even the most important. Moreover, it is no secret that I am against your party.
> Eva: Of course, the whole class hates us.

Certainly, the tone of this last phrase should be interpreted with indignation, similar to the tone Madonna's Eva uses when she sings about high society. In the musical, it is obvious that Eva loathes the middle and upper classes because she could never truly form part of them. Eva particularly scorns the middle class because as a child the middle-class family of her father refused to allow her to enter her father's funeral. The middle and upper classes had told Eva all of life that she was "illegitimate." Even as a powerful and rich woman, Eva continues to feel "illegitimate" and unwelcome by the wealthy, according to Ottino's representation.

Although Eva in *Evita and Victoria* does not talk about what happened during the funeral of her father, one can infer that Eva views the upper class as her enemy. To some extent, the emotions that Eva holds for high society inspires her to seek out signatures for a proclamation that she has written. The fact that she goes to Victoria Ocampo's home demonstrates her willingness to manipulate others for personal reasons. Eva clearly wants to use the influence of high society people, like Victoria, to achieve her political goal of dismantling the very society to which Eva and Victoria belong.

Another aspect Ottino touches upon that exists in many representations of Eva is her desire to be loved by the working class. It is not known whether Eva needed this love needed to continue her work or whether it was for more superficial reasons, like gaining popularity or winning votes. In *Evita and Victoria*, where Eva talks about her close relationship with the poor, she expresses her obsession with this love:

> "Eva: It was more difficult to found a magazine. I got to lift my family out of poverty and get married. I am more important than any minister. They love me, you understand? They love me! One hundred pundits will buy your magazine, while millions of unfortunates with tear-filled eyes listen to me.
>
> Victoria: I hate your style, your language.
>
> Eva: I speak this way. I tell them I love them, that they do not need improving, that they are perfect, that they have been exploited and abused and that will suffice. What ignorance of their kind!"

However, Ottino does not focus exclusively on the superficial aspect of this love. She uses the conversation between Eva and her maid in the second act to show that Eva was not just a person who only lusted for power and popularity:

> "Iris: A fairy, you look like a fairy.
>
> Eva: A fairy. I'm tired of being a fairy, but I've got to carry on, always forward. The poor will always carry on the same, tired, smelly, defeated, but, yes, clinging to the lives of those who abuse them, asking for houses, refrigerators, radios.
>
> Iris: As if you were a mother, ma'am."

It is in this conversation that Eva eventually reveals an aspect of her true personality. It is a revelation that can only occur in a scene with the maid because when Eva talks to her, Eva decides that she does not have to present a show or a false image. The maid, a woman of the working class, is one of the people that Eva has supposedly striven to protect. When Eva says she is tired of supporting her mystical image, it should be interpreted as a genuine expression of honesty. As in the representation of Desanzo, Eva recognizes the symbolic importance of her presence to the survival of Perónism. While Eva admits that she does not like having this dual identity, knows he has to continue maintaining it for the Perónist cause.

The recognition of her double identity is the central factor that makes a significant difference between Ottino's Eva and other representations. During one of the most powerful scenes of the play, in which Eva and Victoria talk for the last time, they discuss this theme. In this conversation, Eva talks about her appearance and the image she wants to have.

> "Eva: Are you sure I have so much power? I'm already moribund, and all of the graces that they impose upon me. I can't think to refuse, to tell them to go to hell, to tell them to let me die in peace, to let me grow back my black hair. I want to see my real face, if only once before dying.
>
> Victoria: Do it. Few would have the courage.
>
> Eva: You do not understand. They want me blonde for all eternity."

For Eva, the question of revealing her true face to the world is not a matter of courage but impossibility. Before Eva had recognized the false image she presented to the world, but in this conversation, Eva recognizes the impact of her image on the future and how it will affect the memory that all have of her. Not only does she know that she will be blonde forever in the memories of the poor, but she also knows that this is a false image that will remain in existence for years after her death. It is as if Eva realized her own myth before death, as well as the consequences of hiding her true beliefs and desires from the masses. In other words, Eva knows that she has created a monster that she will never be able to control, even after she dies.

Arguably, the only work analyzed that truly challenges the validity of the mythology of Eva Perón is that of Monica Ottino. While Ottino does not deny the hypocrisy in Eva's politics, she uses it to show the frustrations that Eva has with herself. Therefore, one can observe something more profound than the purely materialistic interpretation of Eva Perón – one where the poor actually box Eva in the unchangeable image of wealth, luxury, blond-hair, and falsehood. Eva took advantage of these surface features and materials because they lent her the poor's respect and admiration in a way that her "real face" never could have done. In essence, Eva was a victim of her own hypocrisy. The phenomenon of her politics was that the poor loved her appearance, which they linked with the angelic and sacred following her death. They did not mind the fundamental hypocrisy that existed in her lifestyle. They maintained the foundation of the myth and the hypocrisy that, according to Ottino, Eva was very much conscious of.
Ottino's ability to not focus on merely one aspect of the myth of Eva Perón, but almost all of its aspects, is what makes this representation one of the most credible of all. Ottino captures something deep in the spirit of Eva Perón that other representations in literature, film, and theater could not: a more humanized Eva Perón. Thus, Ottino is one of the few writers to have

successfully mixed art and the myth of Eva Perón to create a work that both adds to and demystifies the myth simultaneously.

Conclusion

The continued debate Evita inspires stems from the transformative impact she exercised on Argentine politics. Along with her husband, Evita fashioned a political ideology with a broad political appeal to a class of mainly urban and working-class men and women, many of them members of immigrant groups still somewhat marginal in Argentine politics and society despite their demographic significance. Most uniquely, Perónism managed to become an umbrella ideology for tendencies that elsewhere (particularly in Europe) splintered into extreme right and left. Its nationalist and Catholic emphases gave it a resemblance to the corporatist fascism of Franco in Spain and Salazar in Portugal, yet its strong focus on social justice and rhetorical class warfare against the traditional oligarchy gave it much in common with leftist values elsewhere championed by Communists and Socialists. Finally, its anti-imperialist and anti-U.S. commitments ultimately made Perónism an attractive model for left-wing revolutionary movements such as that of Fidel Castro and Che Guevara in Cuba. This ideological diversity was held together to a large degree by the force of Evita's personality, and after her death and her husband's exile from Argentina drastic divisions emerged. By the early 1970s, street war had broken out between nationalistic conservative Perónists and left-wing anti-imperialist Perónists, a chaos that helped lead to the brutal military junta that took over in 1976.

Although much has been made of Evita's symbolic qualities as a maternal and saintly figure who evoked the Virgin Mary in a deeply Catholic culture, she was also a savvy politician and a highly effective overseer of new social welfare policies. A popular stage, radio, and film actress prior to plunging herself into politics with Juan Perón, she had a prescient understanding of the power of the still relatively new mass media in spreading political enthusiasm and organizing popular feeling into effective action. She proved herself able to harness the possibilities of these new tools as few previous political figures had. She also understood from her previous career the power of public role-playing and was able to fashion a public persona for herself with wide appeal. The conservative traditional political class despised her in part for what they regarded as her *declassé* background as an illegitimate daughter from the provinces who had made it big in what they regarded as crass forms of entertainment. But Evita baited them and welcomed their contempt, knowing that the majority of the populace, similarly treated with spite by the country's elite, would be on her side. She consolidated the support of the *descamisados* (the "shirtless" masses) by spearheading massive charitable projects for the poorest sectors of the population.

Eva Perón's brief and eventful life and equally eventful afterlife surely make her one of the most notable women of the 20th century. As a dramatist and rhetorician, she was able to occupy a variety of complimentary roles in the public imagination. For her supporters, she was both a nurturing, self-sacrificing mother and benefactor and a ferocious and militant defender of the downtrodden. For her enemies within, she was an ignorant demagogue who infused politics with destabilizing emotionality and mob action. Beginning with her European tour, a similarly negative image of her spread widely abroad, in which she was portrayed as a ruthlessly ambitious and domineering virago. The most famous elaboration of this version of her can be found in Mary Main's English-language biography, *The Woman with the Whip*, which was a major source for Andrew Lloyd Webber's musical biography, *Evita*. But even her Argentine detractors would likely not accede to such a trivializing account of her significance. Within that country and to a lesser degree throughout Latin America, she remains a force to be reckoned with in her forceful support of the interests of the downtrodden. The left-wing populist presidents who have won elections from Argentina and Uruguay to Ecuador and Nicaragua in recent elections have invariably invoked her example and her symbolic significance.

To engage with the story of Eva Perón is to consider a political legacy that others might have required a lifetime to achieve but that she managed in a mere seven years before her premature death. For her supporters, the many disasters that afflicted Argentine politics in the past half century are in part the consequence of her inability to consolidate her work, while her detractors see her as one of the primary causes of the country's tumultuous recent history. Whatever the case, Evita is a formidable political leader whose story is unique and astonishing. She is also representative and telling figure for the entire 20th century. As women gain leadership roles in more and more countries, and as issues of poverty and inequality remain, Evita will remain a popular person and symbol across the world.

Bibliography

Evita: The Woman Behind the Myth. A&E Biography. 1996

Barnes, John (1978). Evita, First Lady: A Biography of Eva Perón. New York, New York: Grove Press.

Crassweller, Robert D (1987). Peron and the Enigmas of Argentina. W.W. Norton & Company.

Fraser, Nicholas; Navarro, Marysa (1996). Evita: The Real Life of Eva Perón. W.W. Norton & Company.

Levine, Lawrence. Inside Argentina from Perón to Menem: 1950–2000 From an American Point of View.

Main, Mary (1980). Evita: The Woman with the Whip.

Naipaul, V.S. (1980). The Return of Eva Perón. Alfred A. Knopf.

Perón, Eva (1952). La Razón de mi vida.

Taylor, Julie M. Eva Perón: The Myths of a Woman.